Angelita Izabel da Silva
Erica de O. Gonçalves

ADHD AND TEACHING/LEARNING: pedagogical practices for the early years

Angelita Izabel da Silva
Erica de O. Gonçalves

ADHD AND TEACHING/LEARNING: pedagogical practices for the early years

ScienciaScripts

Imprint

Any brand names and product names mentioned in this book are subject to trademark, brand or patent protection and are trademarks or registered trademarks of their respective holders. The use of brand names, product names, common names, trade names, product descriptions etc. even without a particular marking in this work is in no way to be construed to mean that such names may be regarded as unrestricted in respect of trademark and brand protection legislation and could thus be used by anyone.

Cover image: www.ingimage.com

This book is a translation from the original published under ISBN 978-620-2-04611-4.

Publisher:
Sciencia Scripts
is a trademark of
Dodo Books Indian Ocean Ltd. and OmniScriptum S.R.L publishing group

120 High Road, East Finchley, London, N2 9ED, United Kingdom
Str. Armeneasca 28/1, office 1, Chisinau MD-2012, Republic of Moldova, Europe
Printed at: see last page
ISBN: 978-620-8-15124-9

Dedication

I ask God for the wisdom to be a good mum and to help you be happy and make other people happy. Thank you for being such a complete, spontaneous boy with a beautiful laugh. I love you son and I will love you forever.

ACKNOWLEDGEMENTS

Firstly, I thank God for life and for the beautiful family he chose for me, I thank him for the health and wisdom to get me this far, I thank him for the friends and colleagues he has placed along my journey and for having persisted in these four years of academic life, I confess it wasn't easy, I'm sure he blew a lot in my ears not to give up, after all I had a purpose.

To my son Matheus for being this little boy who, even at his young age, encourages me and has encouraged me on a daily basis. My son was my inspiration for choosing the course and for choosing the subject of this research, since the knowledge I seek is so that I can contribute to the potential development of my child and all the others who will pass through my path as a teacher.

I would like to thank my sister Adriana and my brother-in-law Mauri, who, in the first year, worked with my mum to look after my son so that I could go to college, and who then offered to take my son to the psychopedagogue for treatment, because it was during class time. In this way, I recognise that the end of the course materialised in this research is a collective merit, because without these people it would not have been possible to continue the course and complete it successfully and with good results

I would like to say a special thank you to my sister Adriana, who is the joy of our family, the angel that God has placed in our lives, the person who supports me and loves me with all my faults and who, above all, always has faith in my victory.

To my parents for their unconditional love, for learning about life, for pushing me to study and even to go to university, during the difficulties in which my mum hugged me and told me not to give up. And throughout these four years, my greatest gratitude goes to her for looking after my son Matheus.

To my sister Cristiane who is my inspiration, an example of dedication, the first person in the Silva family to have a university degree. My favourite librarian, the person who helped me understand the ABNT standards, loaned me books throughout my degree and who helps me so much in other spheres of life.

To my beloved nephews Daiane, Bruno and Gustavo and my grandnephews Arthur and Gabriel for their encouragement, for believing in me and for the love that you show - and that sometimes I force you to show ©. I can't forget to mention my beloved Bruninho, who always joked with me by asking me how the class was going, that was the question he hated when I asked him, and when he saw me he would ask me the same question back, how many laughs, how much I miss my eternal Bruninho. Now I'm at the end of my tether and you're not here to make me help you with my dissertation, but I'm sure that in those moments of light that come, it's you blowing in my ear how to do it. My beloved, I'm sure you're in a great place and proud of my victory.

Sabrina and Marilúcia, who have been my companions in academic work, research, internships and many laughs over these four years. My friend Juliana, who wasn't my friend at the start of the course, but who was the person who recommended me for my first paid internship, this happened from the third stage onwards and from then until now we have always worked together. Over the years we've smiled, cried and fought, and at the end of the day we've made up, because that's what friends do. Thank you Ju for everything, and especially for your support when I needed it most.

I also have to mention Ana Caroline, who was the first person I met during the entrance exam and who has been a constant presence in my academic life over the last four years. Thank you Ana for your kind words when I needed them most in my life.

To my academic colleagues for their help, for their words of encouragement, for these four years of joy and sadness, I will never forget the affection they had for me during the tragedy with my much-loved nephew, for their presence at the funeral, seeing your faces made me realise that I did more right than wrong over these four years.

To my uncles and godparents for their encouragement, for always asking me about university and for believing in me. Especially my uncle Gerci, who helped me on my academic journey.

The Faculdade Municipal de Palhoça and its teaching staff who provided the knowledge, especially my supervisor Erica Gonçalves who was a marvellous surprise. The person who realised that it wasn't just a choice of topic, that it was something more, for her enthusiasm when she talks about ADHD, for her warm guidance, for sharing her knowledge and above all for her positivity that encourages me, thank you from the bottom of my heart.

Finally, I would like to thank the teachers I interviewed, excellent professionals whom I have the honour of knowing and working with.

"The value of things is not in how long they last, but in how intensely they happen. That's why there are unforgettable moments, inexplicable things and incomparable people."

Fernando Sabino

SUMMARY

Attention Deficit Disorder (ADHD) is gaining ground in the media and permeating the educational world. In the midst of so much information, research shows that there are gaps when it comes to the teaching and learning process of children in the literacy phase. In this sense, the purpose of this research is to provide reflections on ADHD in the classroom and its didactic-pedagogical consequences. The theoretical and conceptual framework is based on Lev Vygotsky, whose contributions can be used to think about mediation in the school environment. The aim is to analyse the pedagogical practices of teachers in relation to the construction of knowledge for students with ADHD in the Early Years of Primary School in a school in the Greater Florianópolis area. To do this, we sought to understand - based on current scientific literature - what obstacles ADHD causes children in everyday school life and what possibilities Early Years teachers can use to mediate in the classroom. This is a qualitative, exploratory approach, using semi-structured interviews. The analysis of the data obtained points to the need to encourage significant changes not only in teaching practices but also in the technical, administrative and pedagogical staff with regard to knowledge and how to deal with students diagnosed with ADHD, ranging from the physical structure of the school, lesson planning and assessments and the circulation of ideas using digital media as teaching resources.

Keywords: Attention Deficit Disorder. Pedagogical Practices. Early Years of Primary Education. Teacher training.

Summary

INTRODUCTION

Attention Deficit/Hyperactivity Disorder (ADHD) is a neurobehavioural syndrome that "is characterised by an inadequate level of attention in relation to that expected for age, which leads to motor, perceptual, cognitive and behavioural disturbances". (ROTTA; OHLWEILLER; RIESCO 2016, p. 276)

Research in the field of education has intensified in recent years with the aim of explaining ADHD and seeking intervention strategies with students in the classroom. According to Rotta, Ohlweiller and Riesco (2016, p. 342), "there is much progress to be made in legislation and access to pedagogical strategies that can be used in the school context with students with ADHD [...]". Some of the reports circulating in the main media show the concern that has been expressed in recent years about the diagnosis of ADHD, the consumption of medication and school performance as some of the headlines1:

* "Eugenio Grevet talks about ADHD in adults for the newspaper Zero Hora" - Jornal Zero

    Time, January 2015;
* "Fábio Barbirato talks about ADHD to O Dia newspaper" - O Dia newspaper, November 2014;
* "ADHD featured in newspapers" - O Dia newspaper, October 2014;
* "President of ABP, Antônio Geraldo da Silva talks to Estadão about the consumption of

    Ritalin" - Estadão newspaper, October 2014;
* "Drauzio explains ADHD and shows how to overcome the difficulties of the disorder"

    - Fantástico, March 2013.

Against this backdrop of circulating information that mixes medicine, psychology and pedagogy, this study proposes to reflect on the possible ignorance, questions and doubts of education professionals, sometimes caused by gaps in initial and continuing training. In view of the difficulties pointed out in the research, whether by families or teachers and, above all, the learning obstacles faced by subjects with ADHD, some questions guide this investigation, such as: how do education professionals deal with students with ADHD? Has there been initial and/or continuing training for these teachers on disorders and disabilities?

---

[1] Information obtained from the website of the Brazilian Psychiatric Association. Available at http://www.abp.org.br/portal/tag/tdah/ accessed on 3 Nov 2017

What are the implications of the lack of training for their work in the classroom?

How do these professionals perceive the development of the potential of children with ADHD?

Have there been any changes in your teaching practices since the ADHD child's medical report?

The research is based on three aspects that justify the development of the study in an academic context. These are social, educational and personal relevance as justification for the proposed work. The social relevance is mainly because ADHD triggers a series of implications in the lives of these children with the diagnosis, which can lead to prejudice, estrangement and discrimination when living together at school and in society in general. The relevance to the field of education, specifically school education, is precisely because of the possible contribution that literacy teachers can make to strategies that enhance the knowledge of children with ADHD and enable them to access historically constructed knowledge. There is also the personal relevance of the subject, which was the driving force behind this study when my son was diagnosed with ADHD (classification - inattentive) and made little progress in his school performance.

Thus, the problem this research seeks to answer is: how do teachers work in the classroom with children diagnosed with Attention Deficit/Hyperactivity Disorder? Based on the understanding that children with ADHD attend schools and are therefore subject to the teaching and learning process in these institutions, the aim is to investigate the pedagogical practices of teachers at school with children diagnosed with ADHD. To make up this investigative process, we chose to conduct interviews with primary school teachers from a school in Greater Florianópolis on the subject in question. It is believed that analysing the data collected could help to broaden the multiple dimensions of teaching and learning in teaching practice.

General objective:

- To analyse the pedagogical practices that teachers in the Early Years of Primary School use to contribute to building the knowledge of students diagnosed with ADHD.

Specific objective:

- Characterise and historically situate Attention Deficit/Hyperactivity Disorder;
- To identify the concepts, ideas and knowledge of primary school teachers about Attention Deficit/Hyperactivity Disorder and;
- To problematise the pedagogical practices used by primary school teachers in the

classroom for the teaching and learning process of students diagnosed with Attention Deficit/Hyperactivity Disorder.

This is field research with a qualitative approach which, according to Malheiros (2011, p.31) "qualitative research tries to understand phenomena from the perspective of the subject". In the same vein, Godoy (1995) emphasises that the qualitative approach must take into account the entire process throughout the investigation:

> The environment and the people in it must be looked at holistically: they are not reduced to variables, but observed as a whole. Qualitative researchers are concerned with the process and not simply the results or product. They are interested in verifying how a given phenomenon manifests itself in everyday activities, procedures and interactions (GODOY, 1995, p. 6263).

The research is exploratory in nature and was carried out by interviewing teachers from the Early Years of Primary School. According to Gill (2002, p.41) "the aim of this research is to provide greater familiarity with the problem, with a view to making it more explicit or to forming hypotheses".

The **subjects of the research** are primary school teachers from a public school in Greater Florianópolis who have students diagnosed with ADHD in their classes.

The **data collection instrument** consists of a semi-structured interview with previously defined questions aimed at understanding the difficulties and realities of these children and teachers. According to the authors Boni and Quaresma (2005, p.72) "subjective data can only be obtained through interviews, as they relate to the values, attitudes and opinions of the interviewees". In other words, the interview is a process that seeks direct information in the field being researched, "widely used when it is desired to delimit the volume of information, thus obtaining a greater direction for the theme, intervening so that the objectives are achieved" (BONI; QUARESMA, 2005, p.75).

The work is divided into three main parts. Firstly, the theoretical basis from a Vygotskian perspective. The second part deals with the history of ADHD, its changes in nomenclature and its specific characteristics. Then, in the third part, we understand, based on the scientific literature, what obstacles ADHD causes children in everyday school life and what possibilities Early Years teachers can use to mediate in the classroom. Finally, the fourth part analyses the interviews and questionnaires in the light of the theoretical, conceptual and methodological foundations presented. It is hoped that this research will encourage significant changes in the teaching practices of professionals working with children with ADHD.

1 THEORETICAL AND CONCEPTUAL FRAMEWORK IN VIGOTSKI

Lev Vigotski[2] 1896-1934, was a scholar who made a significant contribution to education. In general, the author's works offer important elements for understanding the structuring axis of education. From the perspective of discussing difficulties, disorders and deficiencies in learning, Vygotsky's theory helps to problematise teaching for children with ADHD. To do this, we need to know a little more about this author and his line of thought.

Vygotsky was born in Russia, the former Soviet Union. In his short life he wrote many great works, including a vision of development based on the construction of a historical and social environment. This theory emphasises the possibilities that the subject develops through human mediation (REGO, 1996).

During the Russian Revolution in 1917, Vygotsky was 21 years old and already teaching. In his research, which generally focused on the relationship between teaching and learning, he focused on people with brain injuries, the deaf and the blind [...] He died young but left behind a vast body of work that was innovative and of great importance in understanding human behaviour. (VEER; VALSINER; BARTALOTTI, 1999)

According to Teresa Cristina Rego (1999), Vygotsky believed that the subject is constituted through their social interactions based on the exchanges established with other people. Vygotsky's concern with understanding people's potential gave rise to the concept of the Zone of Proximal Development (ZDP). Thus, the achievements made independently, i.e. the extent to which the child already knows how to do, Vygotsky called the Actual Developmental Level. The activities that the subject is able to do with the help of a mediator are called the Level or Zone of Proximal Development (MOREIRA, 1999).

The possibility of a person's development being altered by the interference of another person is fundamental to his theory. For a child to be able to carry out a task even with someone's help, they need to be at a certain level of development. For example: a three-month-old child, even with someone's help, is unable to walk. He believes that what a child is able to do with someone's help today, they will be able to do on their own tomorrow. (MOREIRA, 1999)

Within the concepts built up by the Russian theorist, there is a relationship in which

---

[2] There are different references to the author's name: Vygotsky, Vygotsky and Vygotsky. The last name is used in this study.

learning promotes development. Vygotsky's interactional relationship between thought and language can help us to understand that through intentional mediation, a child can be stimulated in their development, regardless of their physical or mental condition. Thus, "The child's activity is stimulated while he interacts with the people he lives with and in cooperation with his companions, and only then does he internalise these processes" (ARANHA, 2006, p.268).

Vygotsky (2008) sees object and action as part of a significant principle that alternates dialectically during the development of the subject under construction. Vygotsky was a theorist who contributed - and still contributes - to the process of developing human potential. His theory can be widely used in school education, where the teacher works as a mediator of learning situations, organising the construction of knowledge. In this respect, Vygotsky's theoretical and conceptual perspective is in line with the purpose of this study, which is precisely the perception of primary school teachers with children diagnosed with ADHD.

> If we ignore the child's needs and the incentives that are effective in provoking them into action, we will never be able to understand their progress from one stage of development to another, because all progress is connected with a marked change in motivations, tendencies and incentives. (VIGOTSKI, 2008, p. 108)

The basis of Vygotsky, therefore, points to the need for education professionals, families and society to be able to dialogue, question and share knowledge within a school institution, in order to contribute to the formation of critical subjects who are aware of the process of building their own culture and history. Vygotsky did not develop a method, but with his theory he made it possible to make great progress in understanding the need for pedagogical interventions in schools so that people with or without disabilities, disorders and difficulties can advance in their learning levels.

2 ATTENTION DEFICIT/HYPERACTIVITY DISORDER (ADHD): HISTORY, CONCEPT AND CHARACTERISTICS

One of the first references to ADHD were poems written by the German doctor Heinrich Hoffman in 1865. These poems were written about children's illnesses that the doctor came across in his office (BARKLEY, 2008). However, scientific studies into ADHD began with George Still and Alfred Tredgold, who "[...] devoted special clinical attention to a peculiar condition of child behaviour that was very close to what is now known as ADHD." (SIGNOR; SANTANA, 2016, S/P)

According to the studies of these researchers, 43 children were reported to have difficulties maintaining attention and were described as extremely agitated (SIGNOR and SANTANA, 2016). These studies believed that this condition influenced a defect in the moral control of behaviour (BENCZIK, 2010).

> He noted that this problem resulted in the child's inability to internalise rules and limits, as well as a manifestation of symptoms of restlessness, inattention and impatience. Still noted that these behaviours could be the result of brain damage, heredity, dysfunction or environmental problems (BENCZIK, 2010, p. 21).

In North America, interest in ADHD emerged in 1917-1918, when there was an encephalitis epidemic and the children who survived began to show behavioural and cognitive sequelae, which they associated with the clinical picture of ADHD (SIGNOR and SANTANA, 2016). At the time, scientists believed that brain damage caused symptoms in behaviour and attention.

In the 1930s, studies tried to re-establish a link between hyperactivity in people who had suffered damage to the frontal lobes and changes in the behaviour of these individuals (BARKLEY, 2006 apud SIGNOR and SANTANA, 2016). These children had restricted attention and were considered "socially disturbed". Since then, there has been an academic interest in these events.

In the 1940s, these symptoms were generalised to all children who were hospitalised in psychiatric facilities with some kind of brain injury. It was at this time that the concept of a "child with brain damage" was born (STRAUSS and LEHTINEN 1947, apud BARKLEY, 2008). The authors applied this diagnosis to all children, even those without sufficient evidence of brain pathology.

In the 1950s and early 1960s, researchers began to investigate these behavioural symptoms from the point of view of neurological mechanisms and, according to Barkely (2008, p.20), "questioned the validity of applying the concept of brain damage to children who had only ambiguous signs of neurological involvement, but not necessarily lesions". It was from these studies that ADHD was no longer attributed to brain damage, but the focus continued to be on brain mechanisms.

In the early 1970s, Wender (1971) characterised six groups of symptoms related to minimal brain dysfunction: (1) motor behaviour, where hyperactivity and motor coordination were observed. (2) perceptual-cognitive functioning and attention, described as low attentional capacity and concentration, including daydreaming and distraction, (3) learning, where low academic performance was presented, mostly related to reading, writing and maths problems, (4) impulse control, low tolerance to frustration was noted, (5) interpersonal relationships - extroversion, the author identified excessive independence, obstinacy, stubbornness, negativism, disobedience, lack of complacency, insolence and impenetrability to discipline, (6) emotions - mood instability, altered reactivity, anger, aggressiveness, as well as anxiety and low self-esteem. (BARKLEY, 2008).

In 1975, the US implemented Law No. 94/142 (IDEA) making special education services mandatory for children with disabilities, learning difficulties and behavioural problems.

> It was only after the IDEA was passed in 1990 (and a subsequent 1991 memorandum) that the US Department of Education and its office of special education decided to reinterpret these regulations, allowing children with ADHD to receive special education for ADHD itself, within IDEA's "other health problems" category. (BARKLEY, 2008, p.27-28)

The implementation of IDEA has shown that repetition rates have decreased for children diagnosed with ADHD. According to Signor and Santanna (2016), in the 1980s there were questions about the prevalence of the symptom of inattention and, through studies and research in the area, the DSM III modified the name ADD and was renamed ADHD, revising a series of criteria to define the disorder.

In the 1990s, scientists continued their research into ADHD, fostering a series of important advances related to the functioning of the brain, inspiring the construction of a new interpretative model for ADHD. "[...] genetic research, the neurochemical study of neurotransmitter systems, the analysis of the cerebral inhibitory system and animal laboratory research were systematically integrated into ADHD research." (CALIMAN, 2009, p.138)

In the wake of this, there have been several studies relating heredity to ADHD, showing that it is a disorder of a biological nature (BARKLEY, 2008, p.45). Thus, "even more intriguing, research has shown that if one of the parents has ADHD, the risk for the children is 57 per cent" (BIERDERMAND et al., 1995, apud. BARKLEY 2008). Nardi, Quevedo and Silva (2015, p.24) say that genetic factors contribute to ADHD and that there is a prevalence of ADHD symptoms in families with this diagnosis, i.e. "there is extensive literature on the use of family studies in research into the aetiology of ADHD". On the other hand, Caliman (2009) argues that it was in the 1990s that the diagnosis of ADHD began to be accepted as a legitimate clinical condition, with differentiated diagnosis and treatment.

> This growing acceptance of ADHD in adults continues to this day and will probably increase in the decades to come. It seems to have been strengthened in part by the repeated publications throughout the 1990s of follow-up studies that documented the persistence of the disorder into adolescence in up to 70 per cent and into adulthood in up to 66 per cent of cases identified in childhood [...] (BARKLEY, 2010, p. 46).

With the advances made in the field of ADHD, Stroh (2010) points out that the DSM-IV3 (1994) highlights ADHD as a mental health problem involving attention and hyperactivity/impulsivity. According to Louzã Neto (2010) the term ADHD was officially used in the DSM-IV (1994), which described a list of symptoms.

The diagnosis is made on the basis of a list of 18 symptoms (9 of inattention, 6 of hyperactivity and 3 of impulsivity), requiring the presence of at least 6 symptoms of inattention or 6 of hyperactivity/impulsivity to fulfil the criteria for the disease, in addition to the other diagnostic criteria." (LOUZÃ NETO, 2010, p. 17)

In addition to these symptoms stipulated in the DSM - IV, others appear in the literature such as:

> [...] disorganisation, inadequate planning of tasks, impaired perception of time and working memory, as well as incomplete execution of long tasks and difficulties in observing and recognising errors made during their execution. (NARDI, QUEVEDO and SILVA, 2015, p. 24)

Barkley (2008) points out that it was at the end of the 1990s that ADHD was considered to be influenced by neurological and genetic factors, but social and environmental factors were not ruled out. It was at this time that ADHD was also recognised by part of society for its existence and treatment. Benczik (2010, p.26) assures us that "[...] not all children have problems in all areas. ADHD can vary widely in the diversity of its manifestation and symptoms".

The non-profit Brazilian Attention Deficit Disorder Association (ABDA) was founded in Brazil in 1999 to help disseminate scientific information about ADHD. According to the ABDA, this disorder occurs in between 3 and 5 per cent of children worldwide, and in more than half of cases ADHD continues into adulthood.

> There have already been numerous studies around the world - including in Brazil - showing that the prevalence of ADHD is similar in different regions, which indicates that the disorder is not secondary to cultural factors (the practices of a particular society, etc.), the way parents raise their children or the result of psychological conflicts (ABDA, 2017).

In 2014, the DSM was updated with the DSM-V version, which contains information on the diagnosis and characteristics of patients with ADHD, described in more detail below.

2.1 CHARACTERISTICS OF ADHD

As a neurobehavioural syndrome, according to the DSM-V 2014, Attention-Deficit/Hyperactivity Disorder (ADHD) is classified into three categories:
a) Inattentive (ADHD-D);
b) Combined (ADHD-C);
c) Imperative impulsive (ADHD-HI).

One of the characteristics of ADHD - and there is a consensus in the scientific literature - is the persistent patterns of inattention and/or hyperactivity-impulsivity present in the child's life from an early age. The most common signs of ADHD are when the child starts school and has difficulties with learning, development and behaviour (STROH, 2010 and ROTTA, OHLWEILLER and RISCO, 2016).

> Inattention manifests itself behaviourally in ADHD as rambling on tasks, lack of persistence, difficulty maintaining focus and disorganisation - and is not a consequence of defiance or lack of understanding. Hyperactivity refers to excessive motor activity (such as a child running around) when not appropriate or excessive fidgeting, drumming or talking. [...] Impulsivity may reflect a desire for immediate rewards or an inability to delay gratification (DSM-V, 2014, p. 60).

[3]American Psychiatric Association [APA], 1994.

This is a pattern of inattention associated with other characteristics such as hyperactivity. However, it is worth problematising the cases in which the child appears to be restless, active and fully developed, which are often confused with ADHD. Thus, according to the DSM-V (2014), for the diagnosis to be valid, the manifestation of inattention must persist in at least six of the symptoms described below:

a) Often does not pay attention to details or makes careless mistakes in schoolwork, at work or during other activities (e.g. neglects or misses details, work is inaccurate).
b) They often have difficulty keeping their attention on tasks or leisure activities (e.g. difficulty maintaining focus during lessons, conversations or prolonged reading).
c) They often don't seem to listen when someone speaks directly to them (e.g. their head seems to be far away, even in the absence of any obvious distraction).
d) They often don't follow instructions through to the end and can't finish schoolwork, tasks or duties in the workplace (e.g. they start tasks but quickly lose focus and easily lose their way).
e) They often have difficulty organising tasks and activities (e.g. difficulty managing sequential tasks; difficulty keeping materials and personal belongings in order; disorganised and sloppy work; poor time management; difficulty meeting deadlines).
f) They often avoid, dislike or are reluctant to get involved in tasks that require prolonged mental effort (e.g. schoolwork or homework; for older teenagers and adults, preparing reports, filling in forms, proofreading long papers).
g) Often loses things needed for tasks or activities (e.g. school materials, pencils, books, instruments, desks, keys, documents, glasses, mobile phones).
h) They are often easily distracted by external stimuli (for older adolescents and adults, this can include unrelated thoughts).
i) It is often forgetful in relation to everyday activities (e.g. carrying out tasks, obligations; for older adolescents and adults, returning calls, paying bills, keeping appointments). (DSM-V, 2014, p.32)

Of the nine characteristics listed above, in general, if the child fulfils at least six of them, specialists should be sought to investigate the case further. As for the hyperactivity and impulsivity of children with ADHD, there are a few characteristics to look out for:

a) They often fidget or tap their hands or feet or squirm in their chair.
b) Frequently gets up from his chair in situations where he is expected to remain seated (e.g. gets out of his seat in the classroom, in the office or other workplace or in other situations that require him to remain in one place).
c) Often runs or climbs on things in situations where this is inappropriate. (Note: In adolescents or adults, it may be limited to

feelings of restlessness).

d) They are often unable to play or engage in leisure activities calmly.

e) They often "won't stop", acting as if they are "running on fumes" (e.g. they can't or feel uncomfortable sitting still for a long time, such as in restaurants, meetings; others may see them as restless or difficult to keep up with).

f) He often talks too much.

g) Often lets an answer slip before the question has been completed (e.g. finishes other people's sentences, can't wait for their turn to speak).

h) Often has difficulty waiting their turn (e.g. waiting in a queue) (DSM-V, 2014, p.33)

i) Often interrupts or intrudes (e.g. butts into conversations, games or activities; may start using other people's things without asking or receiving permission; for adolescents and adults, may intrude on or take control over what others are doing) (DSM-V, 2014, p.33).

ADHD, therefore, has its specificities that are classified into subtypes, which identify differences in the profile of comorbidity or impairment. According to the DSM-V (2014), ADHD appears in three classifications:

- Predominantly inattentive (ADHD-D);

- Predominantly hyperactive/impulsive (ADHD-H) e;

- Combined presentation (TADH-C).

In order to classify a child as "predominantly inattentive" or "predominantly hyperactive/impulsive", or even a "combined learner", observations must be made over the last six months. This type of assessment takes place through interviews with family members and the school, if the child is attending an educational institution. According to DSM-V (2014, p. 61) "associated characteristics may include low tolerance of frustration, irritability or mood lability".

According to Rotta, Ohlweiller and Risco (2016, p. 43) "studies measuring the prevalence of ADHD subtypes in children suggest that ADHD-C is the most prevalent (66% of children with ADHD), followed by ADHD-D (26%) and ADHD-H (8%)". The authors admit that the combined type occurs more in male children with a high risk of developing depression and specific learning disorders affecting their academic life.

According to Stroh (2010, p. 90), children diagnosed with ADHD, "over time, feel less intelligent and are often called lazy, which makes their self-esteem even lower". Benczink (2010) states that children with ADHD generally don't pay attention to details, are disorganised, easily forget materials or notices, don't listen to instructions from parents or teachers, are regularly agitated, can't wait or get frustrated when they can't complete activities, whether proposed by the teacher or at home.

According to Barkley (2008), these children exceed their ability to pay attention, have difficulty finishing tasks and, in the case of the "predominantly hyperactive/impulsive" classification, are restless and unable to control their impulses and regulate their own behaviour with regard to rules, time and the future. These characteristics can be observed in children with ADHD and are closely associated with school performance.

Cruz, Okamoto and Ferrazza (2016) argue that the significant increase in psychiatric diagnoses in childhood is due to complaints from teachers, resulting in the practice of medication. For the authors, these referrals would be the solution to the supposed difficulties these children face in the classroom. In the same vein, Signor and Santana (2016) problematise the use of medication in children diagnosed with ADHD, often encouraged by teachers in order to promote the docilisation of the bodies (FOUCAULT, 2009) of these students in the classroom. Foucault (2009) reflects on these docile and disciplined bodies in schools, and how this process has been built up over time, especially in the pedagogical practice of educators.

In her article, Caliman (2008) discusses the controversy caused by the exaggerated increase in the medicalisation of children diagnosed with ADHD. The author discusses that in Brazil there is a lot of data related to the diagnosis of ADHD and the medicalisation and controversy surrounding the rapid growth in the sale of the drug methylphenidate hydrochloride, known commercially as "Ritalin"

> One of the concerns of the current bioethical and neuroethical debate on ADHD concerns the separation between the treatment of attention pathologies and the optimisation of attentive skills, which are mainly required in the occupational and school spheres (CALIMAN 2008, p. 561-562).

> In another context, Rotta, Ohlweiller and Riesco (2016) state that children diagnosed with ADHD do not necessarily need to be treated with medication, the authors explain that "in neuropediatric care, medication intervention is only justified in two situations: if there is impairment in school development and/or problems in interpersonal relationships" (ROTTA, OHLWEILLER and RISCO, 2016, p.325).

3. ADHD AND THE SCHOOLING PROCESS

Studies such as Rotta, Ohlweiller and Risco 2016; Benczink, 2010; Rotta, 2016; Stroh 2010 show that children with ADHD have their cognitive process affected. The cognitive process is responsible for perception, attention, memory, language, reasoning and problem solving, concepts and categories, representations, cognitive development, learning and awareness (BENCZINK, 2010). If affected, there can be real impairment in the area of learning for children in the literacy phase, with specific difficulties such as writing, spelling, text production, reading and maths.

According to Rotta, Ohlweiller and Risco (2016), the area of learning that is most compromised for students with ADHD is writing. The authors argue that "students may have difficulties with graphic aspects as well as spelling and text production" (ROTTA, OHLWEILLER and RISCO, 2016, p. 344). And in order to prevent further impairment over the course of the year, these researchers propose successive interventions in the learning process and throughout academic life. This requires a careful look at the students, as each child has their own peculiarities and characteristics.

Difficulty in writing is due to visual motor impairment, causing a low motor response, which is responsible for the delay in completing activities (BENCZIK, 2010). In relation to the subject of maths, Benczik (2010) reiterates that children with ADHD have difficulties retaining information because they are unable to concentrate for long periods of time, leading to slower calculations, which are hampered by a predominance of inattention.

Children with attention problems often find it difficult to organise hierarchical activity structures in mental processes, which has especially negative consequences for maths activities (BENCZIK, 2010, p. 44).

According to researchers Benczik (2010) and Rotta, Ohlweiller and Risco (2016), children with ADHD are unable to retain information due to their lack of attention, which is why it takes them longer to carry out calculations. They also explain that these children have low self-esteem, and that if they are pressurised to correct tasks, they tend to fail.

> Generally, teachers see a discrepancy between the child's intellectual potential and academic achievement, leading to a rate of school failure. In this way, school performance and classroom work are compromised even with children of superior intelligence (BENCZIK, 2010, p. 44).

According to Benczik (2010, p.46), "inattention can seriously degrade a child's academic performance, [...]". According to this author, poor school performance, together with the pressure that teachers put on students with ADHD, can jeopardise school performance. According to Louzã Neto e Colaboradores (2010, p. 336) "the academic impact is devastating, and it is not uncommon for teachers to believe that these children disperse because they don't understand, when the situation is exactly the opposite: they don't understand because they disperse".

Benczik (2010) points out that the problem may be the lack of information in schools about this disorder and, therefore, teachers have little knowledge about ADHD and don't know how to deal with the specifics of this disorder. According to Benczik (2010, p.25-26) "these children are often identified as disobedient, lazy, rude and inconvenient. [...]. Parents and teachers often feel at a loss as to how to deal with them".

According to Louzã Neto et al (2010, p.346), one of the possibilities for breaking with the stereotype of children with ADHD is that "students with ADHD need to be taught how to learn, how to store and recall information, which is part of metacognitive skills". In other words, the teacher's role is to help the student by planning and facilitating the organisation of activities and work according to deadlines.

To this end, teachers can broaden their knowledge of ADHD in order to feel better prepared to receive students with this disorder and integrate them with other colleagues in the classroom (SENO, 2010). According to Benczik (2010, p. 49), "[...] knowledge about ADHD is the first step in helping children in their educational process", since this knowledge can help teachers in their classroom management and enhance the learning of these children.

> [...] knowledge about ADHD is the first step towards helping children in their educational process. The more informed the teacher is about ADHD, its implications and how to manage it, the greater the chance of the child performing well at school. (BENCZINK, 2010, p. 49)

Benczink (2010) mentions that teachers' experience, as well as their commitment to continuing education, enables them to assess the best pedagogical techniques according to the needs of children with ADHD. Louzã Neto et al (2010) suggest that teachers try to satisfy the curiosity of children with this diagnosis and that oral responses should be accepted in all cases.

Another way of encouraging children with ADHD to read is for the teacher to accept that the child reads while walking, since "reading while walking is a very useful aid for students with attention deficit and hyperactivity. Freed from immobility, they have the ability to think better when on the move. Oral reading is better utilised than silent reading: thinking 'flies' less"

(LOUZÃ NETO e COABORADORES, 2010, p.349).

In order to maximise the development of writing skills, teachers should show children with ADHD concrete models to guide their writing. Louzã Neto and collaborators (2010) emphasise that the teacher can allow handwriting and typing since digital technologies are important tools for helping children with ADHD to teach and learn. One criticism made by Louzã Neto and collaborators (2010) is in relation to maths, where the teacher can allow children with ADHD to use a calculator.

As for homework, the teacher can check the child's copy, as students with ADHD tend to copy illegibly and often incompletely from the blackboard, making it impossible to read and understand at home. To prevent this from happening, Louzã Neto et al (2010) say that the teacher can give them a copy or make it available on a website if the school has this tool, or even reduce the number of tasks and value quality by assessing whether the child can achieve the proposed objective.

Benczik (2010) argues that the teacher's style of interaction can help the student with ADHD since "the teacher, understanding the student's situation well, should seat him in the front row, in classes with a small number of students, and in individual classes, when necessary". (ROTTA; OHLWEILLER; RISCO 2016, p. 282)

> Seat a child with ADHD close to the teaching area, to allow for more supervision and oversight. Look at productivity first (number of problems attempted); then focus on accuracy. Don't send home unfinished classwork. Give weekly homework assignments, so that parents can plan their week accordingly. Reduce/eliminate homework for primary school children (research does not clearly show that homework benefits children before secondary school). If homework has to be given, keep it to a total of 10 minutes x the grade in school. Allow for some restlessness in the work area. Take frequent exercise breaks. (BARLEY; MURPHY, 2008, p. 103).

For this to happen "it is important that, knowing the student's difficulties, the teacher allows more time for tasks and tests" (ROTTA; OHLWEILLER;

RISCO, 2016, p. 282). For Seno (2010), these classroom manoeuvres make it possible for these students to have their differences respected and to feel included in the teaching and learning process. As part of this, the teacher must plan and organise the school environment, reducing as much as possible the presence of stimuli that could take away the student's attention and establishing daily routines and a predictable environment that contributes to the child's emotional control (BENCZIK, 2010). Thus, in order for the child's learning to occur with ADHD is necessary:

> Providing a quiet environment; fewer activities per page; asking the child to check their answers; respecting a minimum interval between tasks; allowing the student to give an oral answer or record it if they have difficulty writing; respecting the time each student needs to complete an activity or test and giving extra time if necessary; setting clear and achievable goals for the student to self-assess tasks and projects. This procedure allows students to reflect on their learning and develop strategies for dealing with their own way of learning. (ROTTA, OHLWEILLER and RISCO, 2016, p343)

Actions like these are important for the development of students with ADHD. This is an association between the structure of the room and the specific intervention.

On the website of the Brazilian Attention Deficit Disorder Association4, the tips for educators page contains some pedagogical strategies for students with ADHD: attention and sustained memory, time and information processing, organisation and study techniques, and learning techniques and metacognitive skills. These techniques can help teachers deal with students with ADHD in the classroom. Some of these techniques are:

> 1 - When the teacher gives an instruction, ask the student to repeat it or share it with a friend before starting the task.
> 2 - When the student has completed the task, always offer positive feedback (reinforcement) through small compliments and prizes, which can be: stars in the notebook, words of support, a wave of the hand... Feedback and praise should ALWAYS and IMMEDIATELY take place after the student has achieved a good performance that is compatible with their time and learning process.
> 3 - DO NOT under any circumstances criticise or point to mistakes as a failure in performance. Students with ADHD need support, encouragement, partnership and adaptations. These students MUST be respected. This is a right! The teacher's positive attitude is a DECISIVE factor in improving learning.
> 4 - As far as possible, offer students and the whole class different tasks. Group work and the possibility for students to choose the activities they want to take part in are elements that arouse interest and motivation. We must bear in mind that each student learns in their own time and that strategies must respect the individuality and specificity of each one.
> 5 - Choose, whenever possible, to teach with audiovisual materials, computers, videos, DVDs, and other different materials such as magazines, newspapers, books, etc. The diversity of teaching materials considerably increases the student's interest in lessons and therefore improves sustained attention.
> 6 - Use the "active learning" technique (high response strategies): work in pairs, oral responses, the possibility for students to record lessons and/or bring their work recorded on CD or computer to school.
> 7 - Environmental adaptations in the classroom: changing tables and/or chairs to avoid distractions. It is not recommended that students with

ADHD sit near doors, windows or in the back rows of the classroom. It is recommended that these students sit in the front rows, preferably next to the teacher so that distracting elements in the environment do not jeopardise sustained attention.

8 - Use visual and oral signals: the teacher can agree with the student beforehand on small signals whose meaning only the student and the teacher understand. Example: the teacher agrees with the student that every time he or she notices him or her inattentive during the activities, he or she will place his or her hand lightly on his or her shoulder so that he or she can refocus on the activities.
9 - Use mechanisms and/or tools to compensate for memory difficulties: tables with due dates for the work required, use post-it notes to make reminders and notes so that the student doesn't forget the content.
10 - Labelling, highlighting, underlining and colouring the most important parts of a task, text or test (ABDA, 2017).

In addition to providing guidance to students and teachers on possible strategies to enhance the teaching and learning process of students with ADHD, ABDA also provides important instructions on planning and developing tasks for these students.

1 - Give clear instructions and offer the student organisational tools to develop study habits. Encourage the use of diaries, calendars, post-it notes, notepads, audio reminders on mobile phones and other technological tools that the student considers appropriate for their organisation.
2 - As far as possible, supervise and help the student organise their notebooks, desk, locker or file important papers.
3 - Encourage parents and/or students to "cover" notebooks and books with different coloured paper. For example: maths material - red, Portuguese material - blue, and so on. This helps with the organisation and memorisation of materials.

4 - Encourage the use of plastic folders to send papers and handouts home and back to school. This way, all the printed material is condensed in the same place, minimising any loss of material.
5 - Use the diary daily as a communication channel between the teacher and parents. It is extremely important for parents to make daily observations about what they see in their child's behaviour and performance at home, just as the teacher can do the same for school-related issues.
6 - Structure and support time management in tasks that require long-term performance. Example: when proposing that a research project be completed within 30 days, divide the work into parts, establish what the stages will be and monitor whether each one is being completed. Students with ADHD have difficulty performing long-term tasks.

[4]https://www.tdah.org.br

> 7 - Teach and give examples frequently. Use sheets for daily tasks or diaries. Help parents, advise them on how to proceed and ease homework problems. Students with ADHD can't be given "tonnes" of work to do at home within 24 hours (ABDA, 2017).

In relation to learning techniques and metacognitive skills, ABDA (2017) proposes that (1) teaching should be done in a clear way about the techniques used for that specific learning, (2) setting possible goals for the student together with their self-assessment and, finally, (3) using charts for planning, organising and understanding reading and writing.

Bearing in mind the characteristic of students with ADHD who are more inhibited, self-control techniques are also proposed, such as: (1) anticipating possible learning difficulties and identifying distracting elements, (2) using audiovisual techniques to signal changes in activities, such as raising the voice, raising the hands, moving around the room, (3) giving feedback to the student, highlighting positive and negative points, and (4) allowing the student to get up and walk around the room or corridor, asking them to pick up an item from the office or the principal's office, for example.

With regard to assessments, Louzã Neto et al (2010) emphasise the importance of objective tests. For the authors, dissertation tests contribute to the distraction of children with ADHD. Tests should not be extended over a long period of time, as this can cause concentration difficulties. Evaluations can therefore be done orally. Avoid correcting grammatical errors. Louzã Neto and colleagues (2010) state that children with ADHD react negatively to the use of another environment to take the test, as they feel excluded and different from the others.

4 ANALYSING DATA

4.1 METHODOLOGICAL ROUTES OF THE INTERVIEWS

The locus of the research was a public school in the greater Florianópolis area. This institution was chosen because it was known that literacy teachers had students or had already had students diagnosed with ADHD. Authorisation was therefore sought from the coordinators, as per the attached document. The school offers nursery, primary and secondary education and works with teachers with a degree in pedagogy or a full degree for primary and secondary education.

The classrooms are well ventilated, with good accessibility, *wi-fi, data-show* and air conditioning in all the rooms. There is a coordinator and two counsellors, and the counsellors are responsible for calling the child's family to see a health professional for a possible diagnosis of ADHD and other specificities.

The school works with handouts and according to the teachers it is a traditional school, and assessment is done collectively and individually. The teachers interviewed are pedagogues. The first year teacher has a postgraduate degree in Special Education and the third year teacher is specialising in Neuropsychopedagogy.

The interview was carried out with four primary school teachers from the first to the fourth year. Three of them were audio-recorded and transcribed according to Appendix 1. One of the interviews in which it was not possible to record, answered the questions via *e-mail.*

It was a semi-structured interview and the aim was to keep the focus on the research problem, without it being so rigid as to prevent it from unfolding.

We chose to start the interview by asking the teachers about their prior knowledge of the acronym ADHD. There was cohesion in the answers given by teachers A, B and C. With regard to teacher D, she was unable to explain the acronym, but answered in her own words what she understood the acronym to mean. According to the theoretical assumptions studied in this paper, teachers need to know what ADHD means. According to Seno (2010), teachers have a duty to know the etymology of the acronym ADHD so that they can help students with this disorder. In the same vein, Benczink (2010) assures us that this knowledge will help teachers look for alternatives to help students with ADHD in the classroom.

Although almost all the teachers answered the question effectively, the results of the interview show that there are still professionals who lack theoretical knowledge about ADHD.

Question 2 asked whether the teachers had or had students diagnosed with ADHD, all of whom answered positively. It is interesting to highlight these answers, as it is clear that ADHD is present in all spheres of primary education, which justifies the growing research into ADHD and the authors' incessant search for effective strategies for students with this diagnosis.

When we analysed question number 3, we noticed a divergence in the answers. Teacher A replied that she can keep up, but she asks the person who is treating the child to have a chat so that they can work in parallel. With regard to teacher B, her response was that she manages to keep up, but that complementing her is often difficult. Her explanation was that the pace of the classroom is intense and that, as it is a public school, there is a lot of content with deadlines. Teacher C's response was positive and succinct. Once again, teacher D's response was inconclusive.

In the case of answer number four, each teacher responded in a different way. Teacher A explained that each student has his or her own characteristics and that through observations the teacher will adapt the material. Teacher B's response was that the teaching and learning process is different from that of other students and that it takes place through recording, explaining that the differentiated technique for this student is to draw their attention to the activities using different colours, to have the child sit near their desk and to accept the student's answers orally. With regard to teacher C, her response is summarised: she claims that the child needs constant mediation and that this is done in different ways and that "the techniques are followed according to the guidance of the professionals involved (neurologist, speech therapist, psychologist) etc". Teacher D replied that the differentiated technique is to put the child in the first seat so that she can mediate him.

Throughout the responses, we can see that each teacher has a different attitude towards children with ADHD, which allows us to reflect that there may be different attitudes towards these students with this disorder. However, only individualised intervention and management will contribute to the educational development of students with ADHD.

With regard to assessment, teachers A and B replied that they are able to make adjustments, but they don't give differentiated tests, while teacher B accepts the child's oral response. Teacher C's response was brief: "Assessments are differentiated according to the report". Teacher D replied that she gives a differentiated assessment, organised with fewer questions, that the font size is larger and that she allows more time for the test. Analysing the teachers' answers, we can see that they have different opinions about the assessment process. According to Rotta, Ohlweiller and Risco (2016), the teacher's intervention should be individualised, that is, depending on the difficulty that the child with ADHD may encounter both in the learning process and in assessment. But what can be seen in the answers is that the teachers make small adjustments when it comes to assessment, and each one has a different method of organisation.

Question number six asks what the biggest difficulties are for students with ADHD. Teacher A replied that the greatest difficulty comes from the family, who hand over the diagnosis and walk away believing that it's only the school's fault. Teacher B replied that the student's difficulty is the lack of interaction with friends. Teacher C replied that attention is the difficulty that predominates in children with ADHD, and Teacher D's answer was once again inconclusive.

Question number seven asked about the low self-esteem of children with ADHD, all of whom answered positively to this question. In line with these answers, Louzã Neto (2010, p. 339) says that "damage to self-esteem is devastating and accompanies the individual throughout life, and can jeopardise their productivity and sociability". Correlating with the answers given by teachers number six, it can be seen that the difficulty these students with ADHD have in the classroom is the beginning of the appearance of low self-esteem in these children.

Question number eight was directed at the teachers. Teacher A said that she had experienced difficulties at the start of her career, but that she is currently studying neuropsychopedagogy and that she takes training courses throughout the year. Teacher B replied that she doesn't feel prepared, that her pedagogy degree didn't prepare her to deal with children with ADHD in the classroom and that the institution itself invests little in teacher training. Teacher C felt prepared and said that her postgraduate course had covered the subject. Teacher D replied that her undergraduate degree in pedagogy and her postgraduate course had little to do with ADHD, but she stated that she seeks knowledge through reading.

Question nine asked about the school's approach to students who don't have a diagnosis, but whom the teacher perceives as having ADHD symptoms. The teachers replied that the school's procedure is to talk to the counsellor and call the family so that the child can be assessed by a health professional.

Question number ten was in relation to the school they teach at. I asked the teachers if there was any continuing training, lectures or workshops that would improve the development of their daily activities at school. Once again, they all answered positively.

Finally, we realise that there must be a commitment on the part of families and schools, and at the same time a commitment on the part of the school to the professional who deals with the child diagnosed with ADHD on a daily basis, so that they can act appropriately in this type of situation.

FINAL CONSIDERATIONS

Much has been discussed about pedagogical practices aimed at children with ADHD, as well as the work of primary school teachers in this context. However, it has been observed that there is a need for a more in-depth look by educators, managers and the technical and pedagogical staff of schools, universities/colleges and other educational institutions in order to promote significant changes both in the way they think and in their own teaching practices.

Chapter One discusses mediation from a Vygotskian perspective as a fundamental element for potentialising learning. The concept of the Zone of Proximal Development is appropriate and applicable to this research precisely because it considers the teacher as a mediator in the child's development. The results show that children with ADHD need to be constantly mediated for their full intellectual development, which implies a constant effort on the part of education professionals to understand and update themselves on this disorder and its links.

Chapter two sought to clarify the history of ADHD within scientific chronological frameworks. According to the research carried out in this paper, ADHD had its scientific beginnings at the beginning of the 20th century. Since then, various authors have researched and continue to research the subject. Over the years, there have been some changes in the concept of ADHD, including its nomenclature. In these new concepts, the disorder began to have new criteria in which attention was no longer a predominant requirement in ADHD. This change took place in 1890 in DSM III, which in the near future, more precisely in the 1990s through publications on the disorder, DSM-IV (1994) made it official and described a list of symptoms in order to facilitate diagnosis. This prior knowledge of ADHD nomenclature leads us to reflect on the importance of these studies for the current concept of ADHD.

Chapter three set out to problematise the characteristics of children with ADHD, such as low self-esteem caused by inattention, problems with writing, spelling, reading and maths, and that inattention and hyperactivity and a lack of understanding on the part of education professionals and classmates.

When there is an understanding on the part of education professionals of ADHD, strategies and management can be used to adapt the environment in which the child is placed, facilitating their performance at school.

With this in mind, it is necessary to reflect on the importance of the teacher's prior knowledge of ADHD. Researchers recognise that in order for meaningful learning to take place, teachers must have the technical knowledge that will help them manage this child in the classroom, thus contributing to the child's intellectual and sentimental development. Therefore, the teacher's in-depth knowledge of ADHD will contribute to the student's full development.

The analysis of the interviews in chapter four showed little progress in teaching children diagnosed with ADHD. Researchers such as Barley and Murphhy (2008), Benczik (2010), among others, mention that there are many techniques for these students to perform well at school. The interviews indicated that there is little or no training for pedagogical work with children diagnosed with ADHD, leading to low self-esteem among the students. According to Louzã Neto and collaborators (2010), educational productivity is clearly compromised by the low self-esteem of children with ADHD. In the same vein, Benczink (2010) emphasises the importance of taking a differentiated view of children with ADHD, since the implication of not retaining information due to lack of attention leads children to have low self-esteem, which leads us to reflect on the sensitive view that teachers should take of these students.

In relation to the question about the initial or continuing training of the teachers interviewed, the responses were alarming, as they made it clear that the initial training in pedagogy did little to prepare these professionals for this approach and that they feel prepared through continuing training in postgraduate courses and courses related to ADHD. Reflections on a possible re-evaluation were problematised by the teachers themselves.

The subject of ADHD is highly relevant today and in the future. This research therefore seeks to contribute to the three dimensions of scientific research: social relevance, personal relevance and relevance to teaching and education in general.

REFERENCES

ARANHA, Maria Lucia de Arruda. **History of education and pedagogy**. São Paulo: Moderna, 2008.

BRAZILIAN ATTENTION DEFICIT ASSOCIATION (ABDA). **What is ADHD?** [S.l], [1999?]. Available at: <http://www.tdah.org.br/br/sobre-tdah/o-que-e-o-tdah.html>. Accessed on: 18 June 2017.

BRAZILIAN ATTENTION DEFICIT ASSOCIATION (ABDA). **Some pedagogical strategies for students with ADHD.** [S. l], 2012. Available at: <http://www.tdah.org.br/br/dicas-sobre-tdah/dicas-para-educadores/item/399-algumas-estrat%C3%A9gias-pedag%C3%B3gicas-para-alunos-com-tdah.html>. Accessed on: 18 June 2017.

BRAZILIAN ASSOCIATION OF PSYCHIATRY. Available at: <http://www.abp.org.br/portal/tag/tdah/>. Accessed on: 3 November 2017.
BARKLEY, Russell A. **Attention-deficit/hyperactivity disorder:** a manual for diagnosis and treatment. 3. ed. Porto Alegre: Artmed, 2008. Available at: <https://integrada.minhabiblioteca.com.br/#/books/9788536314662/cfi/2!/4/4@0.00:57.4>. Accessed on: 11 June 2017.

BARKLEY, Russell A.; MURPHY, Kevin R. **Attention-deficit/hyperactivity disorder:** clinical exercises. 3. ed. Porto Alegre: Artmed, 2008. Available at: <https://integrada.minhabiblioteca.com.br/#/books/9788536314679/cfi/0!/4/4@0.00:54.8>. Accessed on: 14 June 2017.

BENCZIK, Edyleine Bellini Perone. **Attention-deficit/hyperactivity disorder:** diagnostic and therapeutic update. São Paulo: Casa do Psicólogo, 2010.

BONI, Valdete; QUARESMA, Sílvia Jurema. **Learning to interview: how to conduct interviews in the social sciences.** Electronic Journal of Postgraduate Students in Political Sociology at UFSC. Florianópolis: UFSC, v. 2, n. 1, p.68-80, January-July, 2005.

CALIMAN, Luciana Vieira. **The socio-media constitution of the "ADHD fact".** Psychology & Society. Rio de Janeiro. 2009.p 135-144. Available at: <http://www.scielo.br/pdf/psoc/v21n1/16.pdf>. Accessed on: 15 June 2017.

CALIMAN, Luciana Vieira. **Notes on the official history of attention-deficit/hyperactivity disorder (ADHD).** Psicologia Ciência e Profissão. Espírito Santo. 2010, p.46- 61. Available at: <http://www.scielo.br/scielo.php?script=sci_arttext&pid=S1414- 98932010000100005>. Accessed on: 07 June 2017.

CRUZ, Murilo Galvão Amancio; OKAMOTO, Mary Yoko; FERRAZZA, Daniele de Andrade. The Attention Deficit Hyperactivity Disorder (ADHD) case and the medicalisation of education: an analysis based on the accounts of parents and professors. **Interface,** Botucatu, v. 20, n. 582016, 2016.Available at:

<http://www.scielo.br/scielo.php?script=sci_arttext&pid=S1414-32832016000300703&lng=en&nrm=iso&tlng=pt>. Accessed on: 09 September 2017.

GIL, Antônio Carlos. **How to prepare research projects.** 4. ed. São Paulo: Atlas, 2002.

DSM- V. **Diagnostic and Statistical Manual of Mental Disorders:** DSM. ed, 5. Porto Alegre: Artmed, 2014. Available at: <https://integrada.minhabiblioteca.com.br/books/9788582710890/pageid/0>. Accessed on: 17 June 2017.

DSM-V. **Quick Reference to the DSM-5® Diagnostic Criteria.** Porto Alegre. Artmed, 2014. Available at: https://integrada.minhabiblioteca.com.br/#/books/9788582710999/cfi/1!/4/4@0.00:60.2. Accessed on: 01 October 2017.

FOUCAULT, Michel. **Surveillance and punishment**: the birth of the prison. Rio de Janeiro: Vozes, 2009.

GODOY, Arilda Schmidt. **Introduction to qualitative research and its possibilities,** In. Revista de Administração de Empresas, v. 35, n.2, Mar./Apr. 1995, p. 57-63. Available at: <http://www.scielo.br/pdf/rae/v35n2/a08v35n2.pdf>. Accessed on: 26 November 2016.

JERÔNIMO SOBRINHO, Patrícia. **Clinical and institutional psychopedagogy.** Sao Paulo: Cengage, 2016. Available at: <https://integrada.minhabiblioteca.com.br/books/9788522123476/pageid/0>. Accessed on: 15 June 2017.

OLIVEIRA, Marta Kohl. **Vygotsky.** Great Educators Collection. Media and Education. São Paulo: Atta, [?] dvd.

LOUZÃ NETO, Mário Rodriguez. **ADHD throughout life.** Porto Alegre: Artmed, 2010. Available at: <https://integrada.minhabiblioteca.com.br/#/books/9788536322056/cfi/0!/4/4@0.00:38.4>. Accessed on: 11 June 2017.

MALHEIROS, Bruno Taranto. **Methodology of research in education.** 2. ed. Rio de Janeiro: LCT, 2011. Available at: <https://integrada.minhabiblioteca.com.br/#/books/978- 85- 216-2090-7/cfi/52!/4/4@0.00:11.4>. Accessed on: 12 April 2017.

MOREIRA, Marco Antônio. **Learning theory**. São Paulo: EPU, 1999.

NARDI, Antonio Egidio; QUEVEDO, João; SILVA, Antônio Geraldo da (Orgs.). **Attention-deficit/hyperactivity disorder:** theory and clinic. Porto Alegre. Artmed. 2015.

PEREIRA, Isabella da Silva Arantes; SILVA, Janaina Cassiano. **Attention-deficit/hyperactivity disorder in the light of a critical approach:** a case study. Psicologia em Revista, Belo Horizonte, v. 17, n. 1, p.117-134, Apr. 2011.

REGO, Teresa Cristina. **A cultural-historical perspective on education.** 3. ed. Petrópolis: Vozes, 1990.

ROTTA, Newra Tellechea; OHLWEILER, Lygia; RIESCO, Rudimar dos Santos. **Learning disorders:** a neurobiological and multidisciplinary approach. 2. ed. Porto Alegre: Artmed, 2016.

SENO, Marília Piazzi. **Attention Deficit Hyperactivity Disorder (ADHD):** what do educators know? Rev. Psicopedagogia, São Paulo, vol.27, no.84, 2010. Available at: http://pepsic.bvsalud.org/scielo.php?script=sci_arttext&pid=S0103-84862010000300003. Accessed on: 20 September 2017.

SIGNOR, Rita; SANTANA, Ana Paula. **ADHD and medicalisation:** neolinguistic and educational implications of attention deficit/hyperactivity disorder. São Paulo: Plexus, 2016. Available at: <http://anhanguera.bv3.digitalpages.com.br/users/publications/9788592725013>. Accessed on: 16 June 2017.

STROH, Juliana Bielawski. **ADHD:** psychopedagogical diagnosis and interventions through psychopedagogy and art therapy. Construção Psicopedagógica, São Paulo, 2010, vol. 18, n.17, p. 83-105.

VYGOTSKY, Lev Semenovich. **The social formation of the mind**. São Paulo: Editora Martins Fontes, 2008.

APPENDIX

Interview Script

1. Do you know the acronym ADHD? Can you explain what you mean?

2. Do you have any students or have you ever had students with ADHD with a report?

3. When you receive a diagnosis of a student with ADHD, the medical report gives you some guidelines for dealing with this student in the classroom. Are you able to follow or even complement these guidelines? What difficulties?

4. How does the teaching-learning process work for this student with ADHD? Is he different from other children? What difference do you notice? Do you use any different techniques? If so, which ones? If not, would you like to know more about what techniques could be used?

5. How are these students diagnosed with ADHD assessed?

6. What are the biggest difficulties (taking tests, paying attention, a specific situation) for students with ADHD?

7. Some literature/research suggests that children with ADHD have low self-esteem, do you notice this with your students with ADHD?

8. Do you feel prepared to work with children with ADHD? Has your initial or continuing training covered the subject satisfactorily? Do you have any doubts about how to proceed in day-to-day practice with children with ADHD?

9. If the child is undiagnosed but you notice symptoms of ADHD, does the school have a referral procedure? What are they?

10. Do you think that further training, perhaps a lecture or workshop within the institution itself for all professionals, regardless of whether or not they have students diagnosed with ADHD, could improve the development of day-to-day activities in the school?

Interview with teachers from the 1st to the 4th year of primary school.

Interview with teacher A, 3rd year of primary school:

a.   **Do you know the acronym ADHD? Can you explain what you mean?**

      A: Yes. ADHD, Attention *Deficit* Hyperactivity Disorder.

b.   **Do you have any students or have you ever had students with ADHD with a report?**

      A: Yes, I've had two students with ADHD and a report.

c.   **When you receive a diagnosis of a student with ADHD, the medical report gives you some guidelines for dealing with this student in the classroom. Are you able to follow or even complement these guidelines? What difficulties?**

      A: I manage to keep up, I usually ask the therapist who is treating the child to come to the school, we make an appointment and work in parallel. Normally this work has a very good effect, but it also depends on the work of the families at home, so I try to bring different material, on the day of the assessment normally with the institution I manage to make sure that these tests are not stapled, that they are delivered in parts with more time for the children to develop. Depending on the case of ADHD, you get to know the child, there are some that illustrate more, others don't need to.

d.   **How does the teaching-learning process work for this student with ADHD? Is he different from other children? What difference do you notice? Do you use any different techniques? If so, which ones? If not, would you like to know more about what techniques could be used?**

      A: Each student is different, you'll realise in the course of your lesson that one ADHD student isn't the same as another, so you have to look at the characteristics of that student, but normally this material is adapted for that child and they use the workbook. I see that there are a lot of repetitive exercises in the workbook, so I tick the ones that I think are most important to develop and we do the others according to what the child achieves. It's not that they can't do it, but sometimes there's a lot of repetitive stuff and ADHD kids can't concentrate, so it loses interest for them. Long texts with lots of stapled pages don't work either, you have to adapt.

e.   How are these students diagnosed with ADHD assessed?

A: The assessment for children with ADHD, in this case the student I have, he's ADHD and he summarises everything and the image is something that grabs his attention a lot, so I try to do this test with images and the same text. Normally the test is the same, what I do with coordination, I make a balance, even so he doesn't feel different, I take it, I do this test, let's say science, I bring laboratory lessons into the classroom and it happens a lot, he's a child who observes too much. To give you an idea, we needed to study a story. When I told the story in lighter words, this child developed much more than the others, because I looked for a text that was part of his world, it was adapted. One more thing was a trip to the CIC to the Arnaldo Antunes exhibition, and this was exciting for me. All the children were waiting for the guide to do the reading, he wasn't, this ADHD child I have with a report is a child who did the reading of the works in advance and very correctly, the guide was thrilled. So it's all down to how you observe the child, while the other ADHD child I have in the classroom didn't do the same reading, now I think that each child with ADHD has their own characteristics, you'll see that one is more agitated, another less so, one has more attention for the image, another doesn't like it, so you have to see, then I adapt the material by talking to the coordinator and asking them to look at it, and I have a lot of support. When I tell them that I see that they are losing interest, I ask them if I can do it this way and they support me.

f.   What are the biggest difficulties (taking tests, paying attention, a specific situation) for students with ADHD?

A: My biggest difficulty is with the families, because from the moment they make the diagnosis and they accept it calmly, but when they think they have the diagnosis and that's it and they think that from then on they don't need to continue, saying that now it's a school move and not the family's anymore, I find it more difficult, once you're in the classroom, as I said, each child has a different characteristic and you get to know the child and adapt your class to that.

g.   Some literature/research shows that children with ADHD have low self-esteem, do you notice this with your students with ADHD?

A: In many, yes, until the child is diagnosed with ADHD, it happens a lot that they have that label that they can't do it, that they can't finish, that they can't concentrate, while others come with support, psychological support, it's easier. I really like working with them and I know it's not always possible because there's a high cost involved, but the family should come along with a team so that we can do this parallel work, it doesn't have to be for a long time, of course we know that this depends on each professional who takes the child and the child's wishes too, but it usually works.

h. Do you feel prepared to work with children with ADHD? Has your initial or continuing training covered the subject satisfactorily? Do you have any doubts about how to proceed in day-to-day practice with children with ADHD?

A: I have a degree in pedagogy and I found it difficult at the start of my career, so I went after it. Today I do neuropsychopedagogy and I always try to train myself with courses throughout the year. This year I've already done two courses, one of which I did with a speech therapist and which will continue in September. She brings news about ADHD and autism, books and literature that we can use to help us. Because sometimes people think that courses are expensive and sometimes books also help a lot, I always try to read something.

i. If the child is undiagnosed but you notice symptoms of ADHD, does the school have a referral procedure? What are they?

A: Normally here at Imaculada the procedure is as follows, we observe and see that there is something different, we first go to the families to talk and after we call the family we ask for the child to be assessed, then we book a second appointment so that we can get this answer, so things go faster.

j. Do you think that further training, perhaps a lecture or workshop within the institution itself for all professionals, regardless of whether or not they have students diagnosed with ADHD, could improve the development of day-to-day activities in the school?

A: That's a very important question. When you go on the courses, you see the number of professionals in each school. This year, I even spoke to my sister (the school's headmaster) after I came on the course. I was delighted with the marvellous course, you can feel the difference in the way the teachers deal with these children, this has to come from the ground up, from nursery school onwards, so that this understanding continues within the institution. When I went to talk to the sister about it, I said that it was clear that the schools that are looking for it are the ones that stand out today with children with ADHD or other disorders. I see that the difference of having this prepared professional gives the child a sense of security for the reception and also for the family. It would be important for the school, when the family says that the child has ADHD, to call the family to talk to the professional who understands because this will give the family more security and the bond will be formed. I always say that the professional must be well prepared, because the rest will be your practice. Last year I had a student with ADHD at a level I'd never had before, so it was a huge learning experience. At first I was terrified that he wouldn't develop, because he didn't talk, he was more reserved, he had low self-esteem, then the work came together with the families and it was very hard work, because it was a very resistant family with two intelligent parents, but they were afraid to open up that the child had ADHD, that's the hardest thing. I've been teaching for 20 years with this whole process, it was the child who challenged me the most in learning, I was thrilled when the child managed to pass straight away, with the guidance of the coordinator and counsellor was what resulted in success as well. The child had a way of schematising the test, it was instigating, I wondered why he did it, because no one had ever done it, so it's what I told you, each child has their own characteristics and some are more pronounced and others less.

Interview with teacher B, 2nd year:

**1)	Do you know the acronym ADHD? Can you explain what you mean?**

A: Yes, Attention *Deficit* Hyperactivity Disorder. It's a syndrome in which the child becomes very imperative, restless, unfocused and inattentive, due to a problem that occurs in the child's brain and ends up affecting the whole of the child's body.

**2)	Do you have any students or have you ever had students with ADHD with a report?**

A: I do and I have.

**3)	When you receive a diagnosis of a student with ADHD, the medical report gives you some guidelines for dealing with this student in the classroom. Are you able to follow or even complement these guidelines? What difficulties?**

A: I manage to keep up, but it's often difficult, because the pace of the classroom is very intense, we work in a public school that has a content-based approach.

It's also a religious institution that has a very frenetic pace, it's very difficult for me to stop and give all the necessary attention and focus to the child who has this type of disorder, but I try to do as much as possible so that they can keep up with the other students. In my case, I have a student who has severe attention *deficit*, and I often have to be by his side, because if I'm not there he won't do anything, so I'd like to have more help to improve his teaching-learning process, to have this mediation, I try.

**4)	How does the teaching-learning process work for this student with ADHD? Is he different from other children? What difference do you notice? Do you use any different techniques? If so, which ones? If not, would you like to know more about what techniques could be used?**

A: This student's teaching-learning process takes place through recording, I always record. He's not yet literate, so he works with capital letters, I work with the board, with different colours to get his attention and he usually does the activities next to me to record and he mostly responds orally and I respect his oral responses. I encourage him to write and, as well as encouraging him to write, I write underneath what he's written what he's said orally so that he can reproduce his speech in order to write. Of course, it's totally different from other children, because they don't need this mediation and he also has a very difficult interaction issue, he doesn't interact much with other classmates, he's very shy and the different techniques I use are to be closer to him, to listen more to his answers, I really value all the gains he makes and respect his oral responses.

**5)	How are these students diagnosed with ADHD assessed?**

A: Here at the school we started, the test isn't differentiated, it's the same as everyone else's, but the mediation is differentiated, so I explain it to all the students and they do it properly, and those who have a report stay by the teacher's side and I read the question by question orally and respect the oral answer the student gives me, because in this case the student isn't literate yet.

**6)	What are the biggest difficulties (taking tests, paying attention, a specific situation) for students with ADHD?**

A: This year's ADHD student has a very difficult interaction, he doesn't allow himself to interact with other friends and the affective issue is very difficult, he's very distant, that's already a point that makes it difficult, because he doesn't allow himself, he doesn't want to do things. But other pupils I've had had problems with hyperactivity and attention, but they were affectionate, so this side of affection is something we get round, and we give affection and receive it. Then the difficulty ends up being that they don't register the way they need to, they don't interpret in a way that's easy to understand, they often go round and round in their minds to come up with a more succinct answer, these are the difficulties they have.

7)   Some literature/research suggests that children with ADHD have low self-esteem, do you notice this with your students with ADHD?

A: Yes, they look down on each other a lot.

8)   Do you feel prepared to work with children with ADHD? Has your initial or continuing training covered the subject satisfactorily? Do you have any doubts about how to proceed in day-to-day practice with children with ADHD?

A: Yes to all the questions. I think that the pedagogy course doesn't prepare us for what we find in the classroom. I did my course at UDESC, a very good course, with a reputation, but I don't feel prepared for this type of disorder. There are now many types of disorder that weren't there in the past, but nowadays there are reports. And even the schools, I think they don't invest much in instruction for their teachers, because it's a way of continuing training within the school itself, working with the cases that are in the school to make it effective and improve the work with these children.

9)   If the child is undiagnosed but you notice symptoms of ADHD, does the school have a referral procedure? What are they?

A: Yes, here at the school, when we realise that something is different, we call the family, we talk to them, we ask for their help, as it's a public school, we play a lot with this help, a partnership. So we advise parents to go to a psycho-pedagogue, even a neuropediatrician to help make a diagnosis, if we see this indication, and then there's also the work of the guidance counsellor, who tells the parents and guides them.

10)   Do you think that further training, perhaps a lecture or workshop within the institution itself for all professionals, regardless of whether or not they have students diagnosed with ADHD, could improve the development of day-to-day activities in the school?

A: Absolutely, I don't think we're a unit, we're a whole, so at some point in life the professional will come across some kind of report or disorder and it often falls into the teacher's hands and we have to deal with a classroom with all the students, a classroom with indiscipline, a classroom with dealing with content, dealing with grades, dealing with students with disorders and reports. So I think that if the school has a sense of respect for the professional, because we don't know everything, we need training and this will optimise the work of the whole school and qualify the professional.

Interview with teacher C, 1st year:

1)   Do you know the acronym ADHD? Can you explain what you mean?
A: Yes, it's attention deficit hyperactivity disorder. A child who has difficulty concentrating, is very agitated and as a result has a lot of problems.

2)   Do you have any students or have you ever had students with ADHD with a report?
A: Yes, I did and I still do.

3)   When you receive a diagnosis of a student with ADHD, the medical report contains some guidelines for dealing with this student in the classroom. Are you able to follow or even complement these guidelines? What difficulties?
A: Yes, I follow the guidelines of the professional involved. As they are clear guidelines, I don't have any difficulties and I complement them by making partnerships with the approval of the psychologist or any other professional involved.

4)   How does the teaching-learning process work for this student with ADHD? Is he different from other children? What differences do you notice? Do you use any different techniques? If so, which ones? If not, would you like to know more about which techniques could be used?
A: This is a student who needs constant mediation from the teacher, and sometimes the mediation is done in several different ways so that they understand. His attention span is short and he is constantly agitated. The techniques are followed according to the advice of the professionals involved (neurologist, speech therapist, psychologist) etc.

5)   How are these students diagnosed with ADHD assessed?

A: The assessments are differentiated according to the report.

**6)	What are the biggest difficulties (taking tests, paying attention, a specific situation) for students with ADHD?**

A: The biggest difficulty is getting your attention.

**7)	Some literature/research suggests that children with ADHD have low self-esteem. Do you realise this with your students with ADHD?**

A: Yes, because in quantitative schools (grades) they are average students.

**8)	Do you feel prepared to work with children with ADHD? Has your initial or continuing training covered the subject satisfactorily? Do you have any doubts about how to proceed in day-to-day practice with children with ADHD?**

A: Yes, I feel prepared, because I have a postgraduate qualification and it has covered the subject. I have no doubts about the approach, but I'm always on the lookout for new procedures in the field of ADHD.

**9)	If the child doesn't have a diagnosis, but you notice symptoms of ADHD, does the school have a referral procedure? What are they?**

A: Yes, initially it's observation and gathering information with colleagues who also work with the child, and then after talking to the family it's on to qualified professionals for investigation.

**10)	Do you think that further training, perhaps a lecture or workshop within the institution itself for all professionals, regardless of whether or not they have students diagnosed with ADHD, could improve the development of day-to-day activities in the school?**

A: It's fundamental for an education professional, because every day neurology discovers new approaches and paths to be followed in the development of ADHD.

Interview with teacher D, 4th grade:

**1)	Do you know the acronym ADHD? Can you explain what you mean?**

A: ADHD, they're children who disperse, they need more time, many need medication to be able to concentrate, because they disperse a lot, it depends on the case, there are children who are ADHD but don't disperse as much, there are others who have it and disperse a lot more.

2)   Do you have any students or have you ever had students with ADHD with a report?
A: Yes.

3)   When you receive a diagnosis of a student with ADHD, the medical report contains some guidelines for dealing with this student in the classroom. Are you able to follow or even complement these guidelines? What difficulties?
A: It's just that in order for us to be able to do a good job, there has to be a partnership between the school and the family, that's the difficulty, because we don't always find this willingness on the part of the family, at first they're even willing, but then they're forgotten.

4)   How does the teaching-learning process work for this student with ADHD? Is he different from other children? What differences do you notice? Do you use any different techniques? If so, which ones? If not, would you like to know more about which techniques could be used?
A: What I do in the classroom is always leave the student in the first desk, I'm always close to him so that I can be organising, helping him to organise, because due to this dispersion he ends up not being able to organise himself, to be attentive, to be doing what he's supposed to be doing, so I always leave him in front so that I can get his attention, so that I can be organising with him, mediating. Not that I do it for him, but we have to be much closer.

5)   How are these students diagnosed with ADHD assessed?
A: So, we organise them with a smaller number, because they are very intelligent children, at least the one I have in class, he's very intelligent, but he always needs more time. So what we do is organise the assessments with a smaller number of questions and a larger font so that it's easier to read.

6)   What are the biggest difficulties (taking tests, paying attention, a specific situation) for students with ADHD?
A: It does, because if you think about it, one thing goes hand in hand with the other, because assessment is still an activity and it depends a lot on the day the child is in, some days he's super-fine, he can do everything super-focused, on other days he's extremely more agitated, or he's not agitated, but he's calm, but he's totally off, he loses focus, he loses his train of thought,

he disperses more easily, or we think he's paying attention, but his head is travelling.

7)   Some literature/research suggests that children with ADHD have low self-esteem. Do you realise this with your students with ADHD?
A: I see, there's a lot of it.

8)   Do you feel prepared to work with children with ADHD? Has your initial or continuing training covered the subject satisfactorily? Do you have any doubts about how to proceed in day-to-day practice with children with ADHD?
A: So, in terms of degrees, we have very little, what we get is when we go in search of reading, like postgraduate studies, and even then, postgraduate studies alone don't give you much, they give you the criteria, but each child presents in a different way. It's not because it's ADHD, but one is different from the other, so each one has their own characteristics, sometimes for one it's very pronounced and for another not so much.

9)   If the child doesn't have a diagnosis, but you notice symptoms of ADHD, does the school have a referral procedure? What are they?
A: Yes, we always talk to the counsellor, call the family and ask for an assessment, and the family goes to the psychopedagogue to make all the necessary referrals.

10)   Do you think that further training, perhaps a lecture or workshop within the institution itself for all professionals, regardless of whether or not they have students diagnosed with ADHD, could improve the development of day-to-day activities in the school?
A: Although here we don't have lectures very often, but we do have counsellors who are always there to support us, to help us in this sense, to look for readings, to talk to the people who are part of the children's professionals.

Printed by Books on Demand GmbH, Norderstedt / Germany